Thank y

You can personalize this book for your Dad!

Find a special photograph of you!
Simply tape your photo on the corners and place over the photo on this page.
Make sure that your photo shows through the window of the book's front cover.

Thank You, Dad

My father didn't tell me how to live; he lived,
and let me watch him do it.

◆

CLARENCE BUDDINGTON KELLAND

*Just as a father has compassion
on his children,
So the LORD has compassion
on those who fear Him.*

PSALM 103:13 NASB

You do so much, Dad. You're provider, leader, drill sergeant, teacher, and banker all rolled into one. You're coach and confidant to your son, protector and teacher to your daughter. You show us what God the Father is like. For all that you do, you are rewarded with your children's hugs and smiles and are gifted with the symbols of their love for you—the argyle socks, the bright ties, the occasional cartoon barbecue apron. You're blessed to have so much.

This little book is a celebration of all that you are—your wit when your children need encouragement, your wisdom when your children are heartbroken, your bravery when your children are frightened. Dad, never doubt how very much you are appreciated, how much we thank God for you. This little book is a small measure of appreciation for everything you are.

The glory of children is their father.

PROVERBS 17:6 NKJV

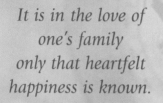

*It is in the love of
one's family
only that heartfelt
happiness is known.*

◆

THOMAS JEFFERSON

Thank You, Dad

Copyright © 2004 GRQ, Inc.

ISBN 1-59475-004-1

Published by Blue Sky Ink

Brentwood, Tennessee.

Editor: Lila Empson

Writer: Jonathan Rogers

Cover and text design: Diane Whisner

04 05 06 4 3 2

Thank You, Dad

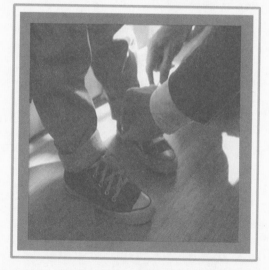

A Collection of Fatherly Wisdom and Inspiration

Brentwood, Tennessee

What can be more clear
and sound in explanation,
than the love of a parent
to his child?

◆

WILLIAM GODWIN

Becoming a father is easy enough,
But being one can be rough.

WILHELM BUSCH

You can learn many things from children.
How much patience you have, for instance.

FRANKLIN P. ADAMS

Before I got married, I had six theories about raising children. Now I have six children and no theories.

◆

JOHN WILMOT

*Honor your father and your mother, as
the LORD your God has commanded you,
that your days may be long.*

DEUTERONOMY 5:16 NKJV

*To understand your parents' love you
must raise children yourself.*

*If you would have your son walk
honourable through the world, you
must not attempt to clear the stones
from his path, but teach him to walk
firmly over them—not insist upon
leading him by the hand, but let him
learn to go alone.*

ANNE BRONTË

One Dad Remembers...

*D*ad, when I was little, I thought you could do no wrong. You knew everything about everything, as far as I was concerned. Then I became a teenager. And like a typical teenager, I thought my Dad was completely out of touch. I thought you didn't understand what I was going through. Now that I'm a father myself, I can see just how much you understood. I was the one who had lost touch, not you. I know you're not perfect, but you might be surprised how often I ask myself, *What would Dad do in this situation?*

When I was a boy of fourteen, my father was so ignorant I could hardly stand to have the old man around. But when I got to be twenty-one, I was astonished at how much the old man had learned in seven years.

Source Unknown

Education is something you get when your father sends you to college. But it isn't complete until you send your son there.

Source Unknown

My mother and father are the only people on the whole planet for whom I will never begrudge a thing. Should I achieve great things, it is the work of their hands; they are splendid people, and their absolute love of their children places them above the highest praise. It cloaks all of their shortcomings, shortcomings that may have resulted from a difficult life.

◆

ANTON CHEKHOV

Except for my father and my mother, everybody lies.

*Heaven and earth are grand; father
and mother are venerable.*

*The righteous man leads a
blameless life;
blessed are his children
after him.*

◆

PROVERBS 20:7 NIV

So live that you wouldn't be ashamed to sell the family parrot to the town gossip.

◆

WILL ROGERS

All your sons will be taught of the LORD;
And the well-being of your sons will be great.

ISAIAH 54:13 NASB

I will instruct you and teach you in the way
which you should go;
I will counsel you with My eye upon you.

PSALM 32:8 NASB

*The richest inheritance
need not come from the
wealthiest father.*

◆

Source Unknown

*Blessed indeed is the man who hears
many gentle voices call him father!*

LYDIA M. CHILD

Did You Know?

In 1909, Sonora Dodd sat listening to a Mother's Day sermon. Her own mother had died, and her dad had raised her. Then the idea struck her. She would show her dad how much she appreciated his selflessness and sacrifices to raise her and her five siblings. She chose the month of June because that was her dad's birth month, and a year later, on June 19, 1910, in Spokane, Washington, the very first father's day was celebrated.

The idea was greeted enthusiastically and caught on quickly. Five years later, Calvin Coolidge gave his presidential support to the idea of a national day to honor fathers. And then fifty-six years later, President Lyndon Johnson proclaimed the third Sunday of June as Father's Day.

Teach your children to choose the right path, and when they are older, they will remain upon it.

◆

PROVERBS 22:6 NLT

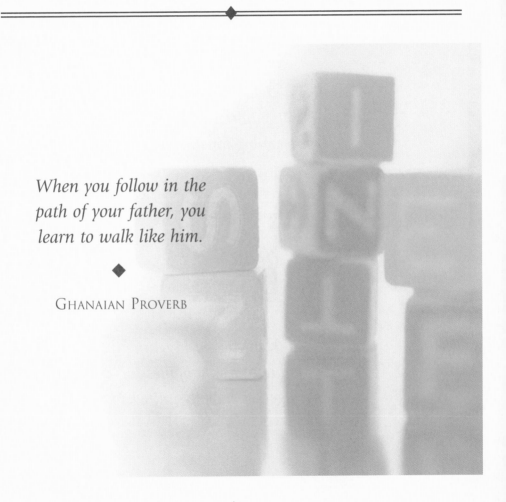

When you follow in the path of your father, you learn to walk like him.

◆

GHANAIAN PROVERB

We find delight in the beauty and happiness of children that makes the heart too big for the body.

RALPH WALDO EMERSON

All the wealth in the world cannot be compared with the happiness of living together happily united.

SAINT MARGUERITE D'YOUVILLE

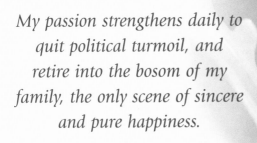

My passion strengthens daily to quit political turmoil, and retire into the bosom of my family, the only scene of sincere and pure happiness.

◆

<small>THOMAS JEFFERSON TO HIS DAUGHTER, MARTHA</small>

It sometimes happens, even in the best of families, that a baby is born. This is not necessarily cause for alarm. The important thing is to keep your wits about you and borrow some money.

ELINOR GOULDING SMITH

A Poet's Welcome to His Love-Begotten Daughter

Lord grant that thou may aye inherit
Thy mither's person, grace, an' merit,
An' thy poor, worthless daddy's spirit,
Without his failin's.

ROBERT BURNS

None of you can ever be proud enough of being the child of such a father, who has not his equal in this world—so great, so good, so faultless. Try, all of you, to follow in his footsteps and don't be discouraged, for to be really in everything like him none of you, I am sure, will ever be. Try, therefore, to be like him in some points, and you will have acquired a great deal.

QUEEN VICTORIA

Survival Tip

*L*ive Honestly:

Everybody wants his children to be honest. The only way to teach honesty is to live it. A white lie here, a cut corner there—your kids notice these things. But when you're truthful even when it's hard, even when there's no way you'd be caught if you did lie, they notice that, too.

Fathers, don't exasperate your children by coming down hard on them. Take them by the hand and lead them in the way of the Master.

EPHESIANS 6:4 THE MESSAGE

A torn jacket is soon mended, but hard words bruise the soul of a child.

◆

HENRY WADSWORTH
LONGFELLOW

*One father is more than a hundred
schoolmasters.*

GEORGE HERBERT

*Don't be discouraged if your children
reject your advice. Years later they will
offer it to their own offspring.*

SOURCE UNKNOWN

Give to a pig when it grunts and a child when it cries, and you will have a fine pig and a bad child.

◆

DANISH PROVERB

You may not be able to leave your children a great inheritance, but day by day, you may be weaving coats for them which they will wear for all eternity.

THEODORE L. CUYLER

The Boatman on the Bridge

*H*e's been saving up to buy a boat since he was a boy. He's had the money, many times over. But he always seems to know somebody who needs the money worse than he needs a boat—a neighbor who can't make rent, a daughter who needs braces, a friend who's between jobs. "I like fishing from the bridge anyway," he always says, but his children know the real story: to their father, people are more important than things. Through the years, he must have socked away enough to buy a sixty-foot yacht. But there he is, still fishing from the bridge. And his children know that no yachtsman on the bay is as rich as he is.

*Children are a gift from the L*ORD*;*
they are a reward from him.
Children born to a young man
are like sharp arrows in a
warrior's hands.
How happy is the man whose quiver
is full of them!

◆

PSALM 127:3–5 NLT

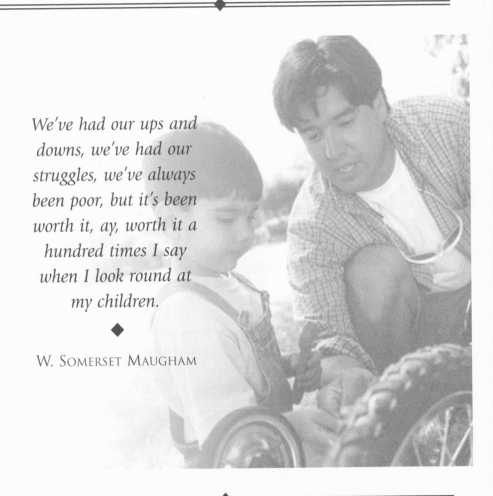

We've had our ups and downs, we've had our struggles, we've always been poor, but it's been worth it, ay, worth it a hundred times I say when I look round at my children.

◆

W. Somerset Maugham

It is a wise child that knows his own father.

HOMER

It is a wise father that knows his own child.

WILLIAM SHAKESPEARE

It is a wise child that knows his own father, and an unusual one that unreservedly approves of him.

MARK TWAIN

Therefore be careful how you walk,
not as unwise men, but as wise.

EPHESIANS 5:15 NASB

Children are unpredictable. You never know what inconsistency they are going to catch you in next.

FRANKLIN P. JONES

A child tells in the street what its father and mother say at home.

THE TALMUD

One Dad
Remembers . . .

*I*t's certainly not a secret how much you love your children,
Dad. After all, you told everyone you knew. You set an
example for unreserved love that was a little hard to believe
at times. But I never really understood how much you loved
us until the day our girl was born. When the nurse put her
in my arms and I looked into her little face, I knew right
then I would never be the same. *This is what a father's love is
all about.*

You created every part of me; you put me together in my mother's womb.

PSALM 139:13 GNT

We never know the love of our parents for us till we have become parents.

HENRY WARD BEECHER

There was . . . a large, shaggy dog, whose nose, reports said, was full of porcupine quills. I can testify that he looked very sober. This is the usual fortune of pioneer dogs, for they have to face the brunt of the battle for their race. . . . When a generation or two have used up all their enemies' darts, their successors lead a comparatively easy life. We owe to our fathers analogous blessings.

◆

HENRY DAVID THOREAU

*I must study politics and war that my sons may have
the liberty to study mathematics and philosophy.*

JOHN ADAMS

*One generation plants the trees;
another gets the shade.*

CHINESE PROVERB

*I will pour out my spirit on
your children and my blessing
on your descendants.*

ISAIAH 44:3 GNT

*There is no friendship,
no love like that of the
parent for the child.*

♦

GOD's love, though, is ever and always,
eternally present to all who fear him,
Making everything right for them and their children.

PSALM 103:17 THE MESSAGE

Be merciful, just as your Father is merciful.

LUKE 6:36 NASB

*A loving heart is the
truest wisdom.*

◆

CHARLES DICKENS

*A father is a banker provided
by nature.*

FRENCH PROVERB

Did You Know?

Ah, the joys of fatherhood. One of them is giving the kids some money—or, if you're really brave, the credit card—so they can go buy you a Father's Day present. Apparently, that habit dies hard, even for kids who have grown up and moved to a new area code. The busiest day of the year for collect long-distance calls is Father's Day. Everybody wants to talk to Dad on his big day . . . especially if he's paying.

*Make your father
happy! Make your
mother proud!*

PROVERBS 23:25
THE MESSAGE

I had a consuming ambition to possess a miller's thumb. I believe I have never since wanted anything more desperately than I wanted my right thumb to be flattened as my father's had become, during his earlier years of a miller's life.

JANE ADDAMS

The best way to keep children home is to keep the home atmosphere pleasant—and let the air out of the tires.

DOROTHY PARKER

Small children disturb your sleep, big children your life.

YIDDISH PROVERB

*No wise man takes responsibility
for an eighteen-year-old daughter.*

◆

<small>CHINESE PROVERB</small>

A Father's Bedtime Wish

Bid a strong ghost stand at the head
That my Michael may sleep sound,
Nor cry, nor turn in the bed,
Till his morning meal come round;
And may departing twilight keep
All dread afar till morning's back.

W. B. YEATS

*It is not flesh and blood, but heart which
makes us fathers and sons.*

JOHANN FRIEDRICH VON SCHILLER

The son shoots a leopard; the father is proud.

AFRICAN PROVERB

A letter from home is worth
ten thousand ounces of gold.

CHINESE PROVERB

Survival Tip

Write Your Kids a Letter:

Everybody likes getting a letter from Dad, whether grown up
and on one's own, or toddlers, or somewhere in between.
Send a letter or an e-mail. Or put a note in a lunchbox. It
doesn't have to contain the wisdom of the ages. Just let your
kids know you're thinking about them.

Those who fear the LORD are secure; he will be a place of refuge for their children.

PROVERBS 14:26 NLT

For unflagging interest and enjoyment, a household of children, if things go reasonably well, certainly makes all other forms of success and achievement lose their importance by comparison.

◆

THEODORE ROOSEVELT

When Charles first saw our child Mary, he said all the proper things for a new father. He looked upon the poor little red thing and blurted, "She's more beautiful than the Brooklyn Bridge."

HELEN HAYES

My daughter's my daughter all her life.

DINAH MARIA MULOCK CRAIK

Certain is it that there is no kind of affection so purely angelic as of a father to a daughter.

◆

JOSEPH ADDISON

By profession I am a soldier and take pride in that fact. But I am prouder—infinitely prouder—to be a father. A soldier destroys in order to build; the father only builds, never destroys. The one has the potentiality of death; the other embodies creation and life.

DOUGLAS MACARTHUR

A Father's Arms

She couldn't swim. But that didn't stop her from jumping in the deep end. Nothing could keep that hard-headed little five-year-old from doing exactly as she pleased. But Daddy was there. He always was. He was in the pool in a flash. Before the lifeguard even knew what had happened, he had wrapped his strong arms around his little girl and brought her to a safe place. It wasn't the first time he had rescued her from herself. And it wouldn't be the last.

*Be doers of the word, and
not merely hearers who
deceive themselves.*

JAMES 1:22 NRSV

Hypocrisy in anything whatever may deceive the cleverest and most penetrating man, but the least wide-awake of children recognizes it, and is revolted by it, however ingeniously it may be disguised.

LEO TOLSTOY

*Gold or silver mansions are not as good
as one's own thatched house.*

CHINESE PROVERB

A man's house is his castle.

SIR EDWARD COKE

'Mid pleasures and palaces though we may roam,
Be it ever so humble, there's no place like home.

JOHN HOWARD PAINE

Never forget these commands that I am giving you today. Teach them to your children. Repeat them when you are at home and when you are away, when you are resting and when you are working.

DEUTERONOMY 6:6–7 GNT

Our lips shall tell them to our sons,
And they again to theirs;
That generations yet unborn
May teach them to their heirs.

ISAAC WATTS

When you teach your son, you
teach your son's son.

THE TALMUD

One Dad Remembers . . .

When I was five, I begged and begged for a BB gun, but you wouldn't give me one. I was furious at the time. I couldn't understand why you would refuse me something I wanted so badly. Now that I'm a father myself, I understand why you wouldn't give it to me. Thanks, Dad, for protecting me from myself.

*Hear, my child, your father's instruction,
and reject not your mother's teaching.*

PROVERBS 1:8 NRSV

Rashness belongs to youth; prudence to old age.

CICERO

I wish thee, Vin, before all wealth,
Both bodily and ghostly health;
Nor too much wealth, nor wit, come to thee,
So much of either may undo thee.
I wish thee learning, not for show,
Enough for to instruct and know . . .
I wish thee peace in all thy ways,
Nor lazy nor contentious days;
And when thy soul and body part,
As innocent as now thou art.

◆

RICHARD CORBET TO HIS SON, VINCENT

O may she live like some green laurel
Rooted in one dear perpetual place.

W. B. YEATS ABOUT HIS DAUGHTER

Son, brother, father, lover, friend. There is room
in the heart for all the affections, as there is room
in heaven for all the stars.

VICTOR HUGO

Make our sons in their prime
like sturdy oak trees,
Our daughters as shapely and bright
as fields of wildflowers.

◆

Psalm 144:12 the message

Blest the man whose age is cheered
By stalwart sons and daughters fair;
No enemies by him are feared,
No lack of love, no want of care.

◆

THE PSALTER (1912)

Stockpile treasure in heaven, where it's safe from moths and rust and burglars. It's obvious, isn't it? The place where your treasure is, is the place you will most want to be, and end up being.

MATTHEW 6:20–21 THE MESSAGE

Tell them to do good, to do a lot of good things, to be generous, and to share. By doing this they store up a treasure for themselves which is a good foundation for the future. In this way they take hold of what life really is.

1 TIMOTHY 6:18–19 GOD'S WORD

He who is taught to live upon little owes more to his father's wisdom than he who has a great deal left him does to his father's care.

WILLIAM PENN

*The baby is not yet born, and yet
you say that his nose is like
his grandfather's.*

INDIAN PROVERB

Did You Know?

*I*t can be tough being a father, but at least you aren't the one who has to give birth. Unless, of course, you're a seahorse dad. The male seahorse has a "brood pouch" where eggs from the female are deposited and fertilized. He carries the fertilized eggs for about a month. Then, when the baby seahorses are hatched and ready to swim on their own, he ejects them from the brood pouch.

Children, obey your parents
in the Lord, for this is right.

◆

Ephesians 6:1 NASB

The ship that will not obey the helm must obey the rocks.

◆

ENGLISH PROVERB

The family is the school of duties . . . founded on love.

FELIX ADLER

To be happy at home is the ultimate result of all ambition.

SAMUEL JOHNSON

A happy family is but an earlier heaven.

◆

JOHN BOWRING

Sleep and rest, sleep and rest,
Father will come to thee soon;
Rest, rest, on mother's breast,
Father will come to thee soon;
Father will come to his babe in the nest,
Silver sails all out of the west
Under the silver moon:
Sleep, my little one, sleep,
my pretty one, sleep.

◆

ALFRED, LORD TENNYSON

Children are poor men's riches.

Little children are still the symbol of the eternal marriage between love and duty.

GEORGE ELIOT

My father knows the proper way
The nation should be run;
He tells us children every day
Just what should now be done.
He knows the way to fix the trusts,
He has a simple plan;
But if the furnace needs repairs,
We have to hire a man.

EDGAR ALBERT GUEST

Survival Tip

Get Your Kids to Help with a Home Maintenance Project:

Children love to be grown up and help Dad. And one of the
best things a father can do for his children is to let them help
fix a leaky faucet or put air in the tires. Not only will they feel
like they are making a contribution, but they will also be
learning. At the same time, this gives an excellent opportunity
to talk with them and grow closer.

*A wise child loves
discipline, but a scoffer
does not listen to rebuke.*

PROVERBS 13:1 NRSV

That's the way of a Father. To teach and inspire his children to do good of their own free will rather than fear of somebody else. That's the difference between a slave's Master and a child's Father.

◆

Terence

My son, observe the postage stamp! Its usefulness depends upon its ability to stick to one thing until it gets there.

HENRY WHEELER SHAW

I heard my father say he never knew a piece of land to run away or break.

JOHN ADAMS

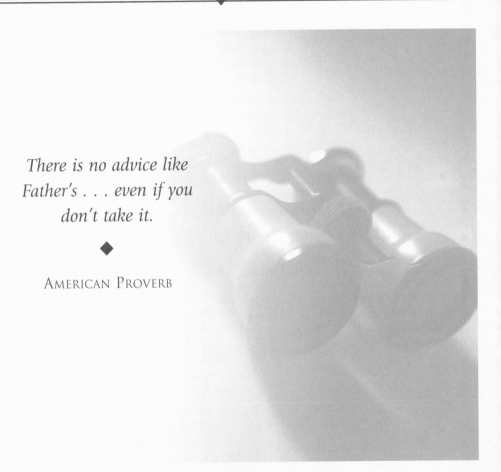

*There is no advice like
Father's . . . even if you
don't take it.*

◆

AMERICAN PROVERB

Only two things matter in this world: a son and a daughter.

The Secret

Two men sat watching three children jump on a trampoline. The younger man turned toward the older. "Dad, you didn't have it all figured out, did you?"

"Excuse me?" asked his father.

The young man gestured toward the kids on the trampoline. "They think I know exactly what I'm doing. They have no idea I figure things out one day at a time. I always wish I had your wisdom. But it just occurred to me, you were making it up as you went along too, weren't you?"

The older man winked at his son. "The secret's out," he said. "Nobody's got fatherhood all figured out." Then a broad grin broke out on his face. "But let's don't tell them."

The goodness of the father reaches higher than a mountain. That of the mother goes deeper than the ocean.

◆

<small>JAPANESE PROVERB</small>

Your descendants will become
well-known all over.
Your children in foreign countries
Will be recognized at once
as the people I have blessed.

◆

Isaiah 61:9 the message

A tree is known by its fruit; a man by his deeds. A good deed is never lost; he who sows courtesy reaps friendship, and he who plants kindness gathers love.

SAINT BASIL

There was never a person who did anything worth doing that did not receive more than he gave.

HENRY WARD BEECHER

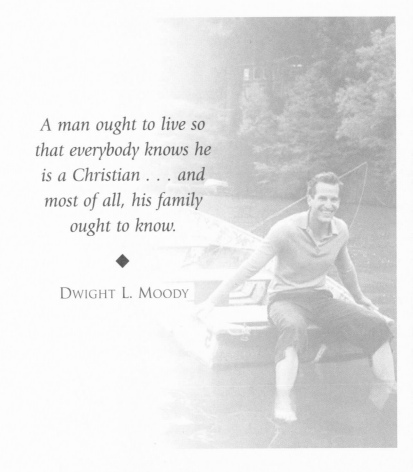

A man ought to live so that everybody knows he is a Christian . . . and most of all, his family ought to know.

♦

DWIGHT L. MOODY

When the time drew near for David to die,
he gave a charge to Solomon his son. . . .
"Be strong, show yourself a man, and
observe what the LORD your God requires:
Walk in his ways, and keep his decrees and
commands . . . so that you may
prosper in all that you do.

1 KINGS 2:1–3 NIV

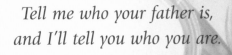

*Tell me who your father is,
and I'll tell you who you are.*

FILIPINO PROVERB

Noble fathers have noble children.

EURIPIDES

One Dad
Remembers . . .

You always came home from work exhausted, Dad. I'm sure all you wanted to do was sit down and relax for a few minutes. But every time you got situated in your Papa Bear chair, you had us kids climbing on you like monkeys, diving off the chair arms, rattling your newspaper. Still, as tired as you were, you never had an unkind word for any of us. There was never any doubt: as much as you would have loved a little quiet, you loved your children more. Any time I'm tempted to send my kids out of the room so I can get a little peace, I think about you, Dad, and your seemingly infinite patience.

*Govern a family as you would fry a
small fish—very gently.*

CHINESE PROVERB

*Fathers, provoke not your children to
anger, lest they be discouraged.*

COLOSSIANS 3:21 NKJV

You have never by a word or a deed given me one moment's uneasiness; on the contrary I have felt perpetual gratitude to heaven for having given me, in you, a source of so much pure and unmixed happiness.

THOMAS JEFFERSON TO
HIS DAUGHTER, MARY

You have begot me, bred me, loved me. I
Return those duties back as are right fit,
Obey you, love you, and most honor you.

CORDELIA TO HER FATHER IN
SHAKESPEARE'S *KING LEAR*

To a father growing old nothing is
dearer than a daughter.

EURIPIDES

*I will speak to you in a parable.
I will teach you hidden lessons
from our past—stories we have
heard and know, stories our
ancestors handed down to us.
We will not hide these truths
from our children but will tell the
next generation about the
glorious deeds of the L*ORD.
*We will tell of his power and the
mighty miracles he did.*

◆

PSALM 78:2–4 NLT

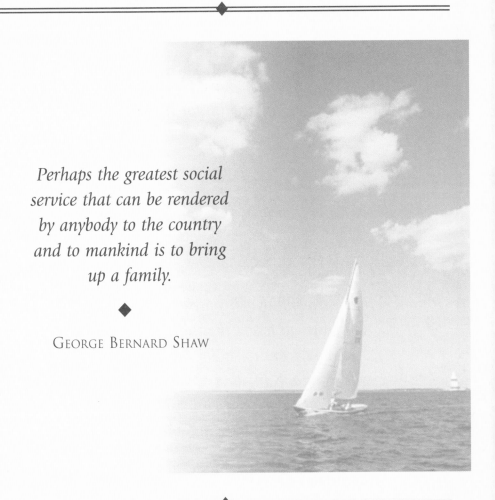

Perhaps the greatest social service that can be rendered by anybody to the country and to mankind is to bring up a family.

◆

GEORGE BERNARD SHAW

You still the hunger of those you cherish;
their sons have plenty,
and they store up wealth for their children.

PSALM 17:14 NIV

Take care and watch yourselves closely, so
as neither to forget the things that your
eyes have seen nor to let them slip from
your mind all the days of your life; make
them known to your children and your
children's children.

DEUTERONOMY 4:9 NRSV

*The fathers of families
have as truly the charge
of the souls in those
families, as pastors have
of the churches.*

◆

THOMAS MANTON

Gerald, you should learn how to tie your tie better. Sentiment is all very well for the buttonhole. But the essential thing for a necktie is style. A well-tied tie is the first serious step in life.

LORD ILLINGWORTH IN OSCAR WILDE'S
A WOMAN OF NO IMPORTANCE

Did You Know?

*T*he most popular Father's Day gift? You guessed it: the necktie. In spite of relaxed dress codes everywhere from work to church, ties still head the list of gifts for Dad on his special day, according to a 2003 press release from the Census Bureau.

If any of you lacks wisdom, let him ask of God, who gives to all liberally and without reproach, and it will be given to him.

JAMES 1:5 NKJV

Wisdom is the reward you get for a lifetime of listening when you would rather have talked.

◆

Mark Twain

*There is little success where there
is little laughter.*

ANDREW CARNEGIE

*Every thing in this world, said my father, is big
with jest—and has wit in it, and instruction
too—if we can but find it out.*

LAURENCE STERNE

A little child, a limber elf,
Singing, dancing to itself,
A fairy thing with red round cheeks,
That always finds, and never seeks,
Makes such a vision to the sight
As fills a father's eyes with light.

◆

SAMUEL TAYLOR COLERIDGE

It ought to be lovely to be old
to be full of the peace that
comes of experience and
wrinkled ripe fulfilment. . . .
And a young man should think: By Jove
my father has faced all weathers,
but it's been a life!

◆

D. H. LAWRENCE

No person was ever honored for what he received.
Honor has been the reward for what he gave.

CALVIN COOLIDGE

Everyone who has ever done a kind deed for us, or
spoken one word of encouragement to us, has entered
into the makeup of our character and of our
thoughts, as well as our success.

GEORGE BURTON ADAMS

*Family jokes, though rightly cursed
by strangers, are the bond that keeps
most families alive.*

STELLA BENSON

Survival Tip

*T*ell Family Stories:

Storytelling is a great way to cultivate a sense of family history. You don't have to be a master storyteller to give your children a real and vibrant sense of where they came from. Tell them about the oldest relatives you ever knew. What did they do for a living? What difficulties did they have to overcome? Tell your children about family traditions: How did your family celebrate holidays when you were growing up? Who had nicknames in your family, and how did they get them? On birthdays, tell your children what happened the day they were born. Every family needs its own traditions, its own little inside jokes. Besides giving family members a sense of belonging, it also helps them feel that their family is special and different from the world outside.

A wise son makes a glad father,
But a foolish son is the grief of
his mother.

PROVERBS 10:1 NKJV

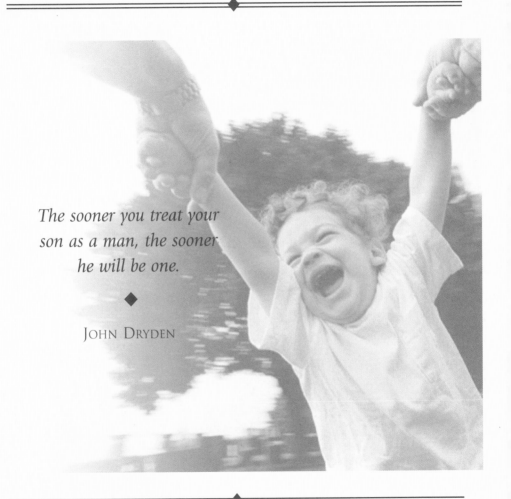

The sooner you treat your
son as a man, the sooner
he will be one.

◆

JOHN DRYDEN

Friendship reminds us of fathers.

MALAGASY PROVERB

Be kind to thy father, for when thou wert young,
Who loved thee so fondly as he?
He caught the first accents that fell from thy tongue,
And joined in thy innocent glee.

MARGARET COURTNEY

*You can buy everything,
except a father and a
mother.*

TAMIL PROVERB